J.S. BACH

Two-Part Inventions and Other Mast[erworks] for Two Trumpets

PLAYBACK+

Speed • Pitch • Balance • Loop

To access audio visit:
www.halleonard.com/mylibrary
Enter Code
2939-0741-3726-5920

ISBN 978-0-98967-055-5

Music Minus One

Exclusively Distributed By
Hal•Leonard®

© 2013 MMO Music Group, Inc.
All Rights Reserved

Visit Hal Leonard Online at
www.halleonard.com

Contact us:
Hal Leonard
7777 West Bluemound Road
Milwaukee, WI 53213
Email: info@halleonard.com

In Europe, contact:
Hal Leonard Europe Limited
42 Wigmore Street
Marylebone, London, W1U 2RN
Email: info@halleonardeurope.com

In Australia, contact:
Hal Leonard Australia Pty. Ltd.
4 Lentara Court
Cheltenham, Victoria, 3192 Australia
Email: info@halleonard.com.au

Gavotte in E flat Major

Edited by Robert Zottola

J.S. Bach

♩ = 150

6 Click
count-off
1234/12

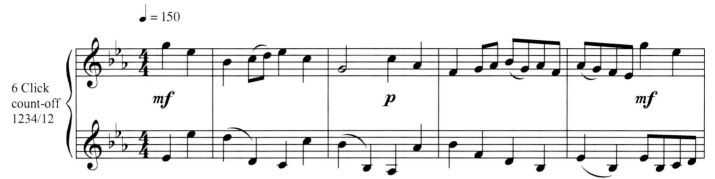

Little Prelude in C Major

Edited by Robert Zottola

J.S. Bach

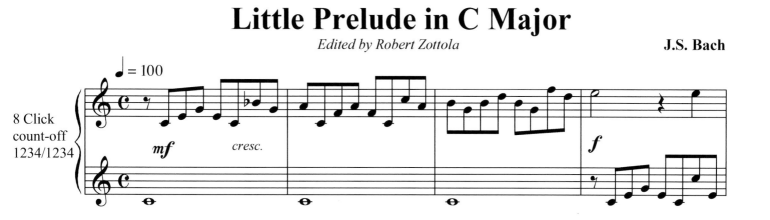

Gavotte in G minor

Edited by Robert Zottola

J.S. Bach

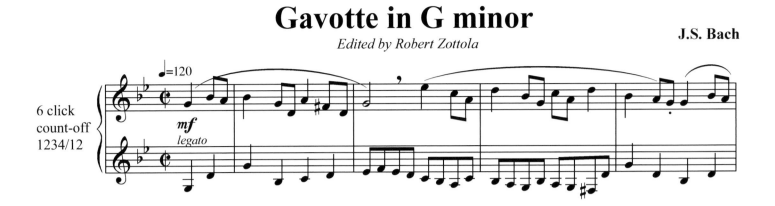

6 click
count-off
1234/12

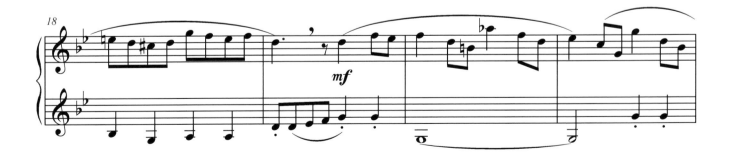

Gavotte in G minor

MMO 6847

Invention #1
in C Major
Edited by Robert Zottola

J.S. Bach

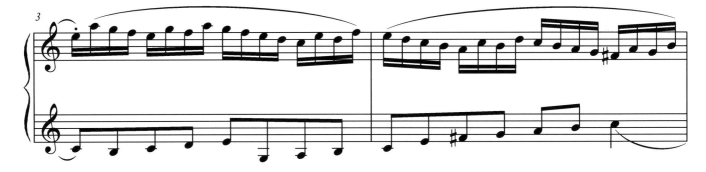

MMO 6847

Invention #1

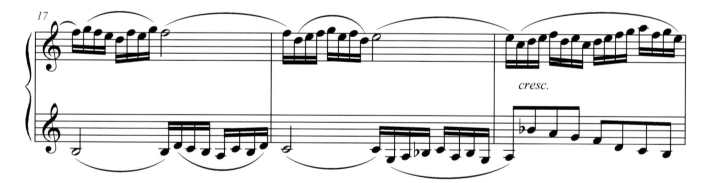

MMO 6847

Invention # 4
in D minor

J.S. Bach

Edited by Robert Zottola

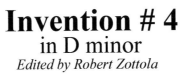

6 Click
count-off
123/123

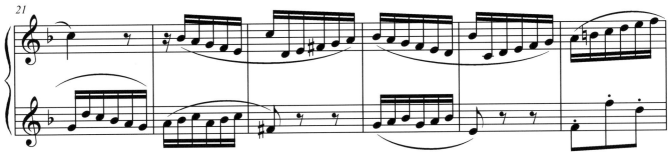

MMO 6847

Invention # 4

MMO 6847

Minuet # 3 in D minor

Edited by Robert Zottola

J.S. Bach

MMO 6847

Minuet in A minor

Edited by Robert Zottola

J.S. Bach

Minuet in C minor

Edited by Robert Zottola

J.S. Bach

Minuet in D minor

Edited by Robert Zottola

J.S. Bach

MMO 6847

Minuet in E Major

Edited by Robert Zottola

J.S. Bach

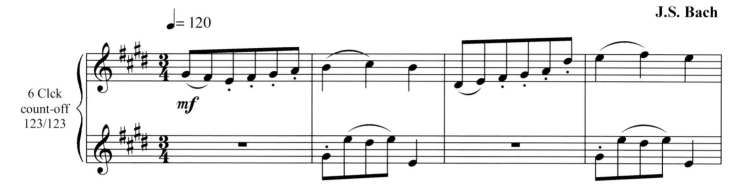

MMO 6847

Minuet in F Major

Edited by Robert Zottola

J.S. Bach

How to Get the Most Benefit and Enjoyment From This Album?

Based on your level of ability, you might want to practice these duets without the play-along recordings first to get familiar with the parts and play them slowly if necessary. In some duets, it might be better to play the second parts before the first. Usually they are easier, although as mentioned earlier navigating through the low register can be difficult so it's not a hard and fast rule. Remember, the inclusion of the click track is there to promote accuracy and synchronization but when playing with another live player you should add the aforementioned artistic approach which is not completely compatible with metrononomic time. In other words, the precision and complexity of Bach's music should not be approached mechanically.

What Is the Artistic Approach?

A short list of the finishing touches to any piece of music...

Dynamics, accents, articulations, phrasing, *accelerando, ritardando* and an all-encompassing musical term *cantabile*. Even in Bach's 1732 copy of *Inventions and Sinfonias* he recommended *Cantabile*, in a singing style, speech-like rather than uniformly smooth.

To Breathe or Not to Breathe...?

That is the question. Not trying to be clever with this but...

Since these pieces were not written for trumpet, finding where to breathe is challenging. With that said, feel free to omit a note or cut it short in order to catch a breath or even a sniff. With smart practice these duets will train you to conserve air and in fact they are a great exercise for breath-control. The eventual goal is to think of the phrases and sections the way we speak with no attention on breathing. Also, Since the form of these pieces often requires repeated sections, it's okay to rest if needed on the repeat and then re-enter. Eventually, you will pace yourself to the demand.

Was Bach One of the Greatest Improvisors?

It's probably a fair assumption that he would be in a class with the great jazz pianist Art Tatum based on, if nothing else his Goldberg Variations and the *Adagio* from the Italian Concerto. Check out Glenn Gould's masterful recordings of these pieces on YouTube. So, as jazz players there's so much to learn from Bach on how to take an existing melody or chord structure and manipulate it in infinite ways!

Why Have a Click Track?

A metronome or click track are only tools to help synchronize and guide you to play with "good time" which simply means not speeding up or slowing down, playing behind or ahead of the beat unintentionally. (Of course, sometimes it may be okay to do either.) But what if you want to perform or record these duets with the play-along tracks? You probably would prefer not to have a click throughout, right?

With the online audio, each duet has five versions: complete, minus 1st trumpet with and without clicks, and minus 2nd trumpet with and without clicks.

And here's an interesting side-note: If you are a "late-comer" to the study of J.S. Bach's music, know that you are in very good company for both Mozart and Beethoven discovered and studied in great depth his amazing fugues quite late in their careers. This is clearly evident in their later compositions.

Finally, the study of **Bach's Two-Part Inventions** and even his simpler pieces serve as a primer for the performance of contrapuntal tonal music. I only hope you learn as much as I did from making this volume while getting the pure enjoyment from playing his inspired works!

I welcome your questions and comments on any aspect of this volume, my humble offering of the great master's music.

Robert Zottola
bobzottola@naplesjazzlovers.com
Naples, Florida.